I0813376

THIS JOURNAL
BELONGS TO:

____

THE LITTLE DREAM JOURNAL

THE LITTLE DREAM JOURNAL

Daily Reflections for a Better Night's Sleep

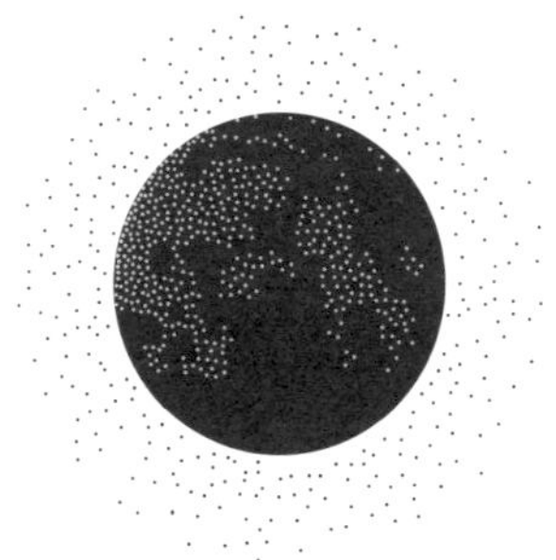

MANDALA

San Rafael Los Angeles London

THIS GUIDED JOURNAL IS DESIGNED TO HELP YOU EXPLORE THE RICH WORLD OF YOUR DREAMS, REFLECT ON THEIR DEEPER MEANINGS, AND GAIN VALUABLE INSIGHTS INTO YOUR SUBCONSCIOUS MIND.

Dreams are more than just random images and sensations from a restless mind—they are windows into our subconscious, where our thoughts, emotions, fears, and desires express themselves.

As you begin to regularly log your dreams in this journal, you will soon start to identify recurring patterns, themes, and symbols that can help you gain clarity about your life, your relationships, and even your own inner struggles or aspirations. For example, a dream about being chased could reveal anxieties you may be avoiding, while a dream of flying might represent feelings of freedom or ambition. Over time, the patterns that emerge from your dreams can guide you toward greater self-awareness and personal growth.

HOW TO USE THIS JOURNAL

Try to record your dreams immediately upon waking up, while the details are still fresh in your mind. Even if you can't remember everything, write down the pieces and emotions that you do recall. Don't worry about making things perfect or completely coherent; just focus on getting the essence of the dream onto the page.

In addition to freewriting space for recording your dreams, this journal includes guided prompts to help you dig deeper into the meaning of your dreams by identifying symbols, exploring your emotional responses, and linking patterns in your dreams to your daily activities. As you complete each entry, take time to reflect on how the dream might connect to your waking life. How does it reflect your current emotional state, recent experiences, or unresolved issues?

Interpreting your dreams is an ongoing process of introspection and self-discovery. You can consult resources that provide common dream meanings, such as *The Little Dream Dictionary*, as a starting point. While some symbols have universal meanings, your dreams are unique to you, and only you will fully understand their personal significance. Trust your intuition. The more you reflect on your dreams, the more you'll learn about yourself and the way your mind works.

In addition to providing valuable insights into your inner world, recording your dreams on a regular basis can also promote more restful sleep. Logging and reflecting on your dreams promotes a sense of closure and understanding around them, which can ease any lingering anxieties. Writing in this journal each morning can become part of a calming routine, allowing you to process your thoughts and feelings in a way that promotes emotional balance and relaxation. Enjoy the journey into your subconscious and allow your dreams to reveal the wisdom within.

RECORD

DATE ___/___/___ SLEPT FROM ___:___-___:___

LAST NIGHT I DREAMT . . .

REFLECT

I THINK THIS DREAM MEANS . . .

3 PEOPLE WHO WERE IN MY DREAM:

THIS DREAM MADE ME FEEL:

- ☐ happy
- ☐ angry
- ☐ sad
- ☐ confused
- ☐ scared
- ☐ other

HOW DOES THIS DREAM RELATE TO MY LIFE?

RATING MY QUALITY OF SLEEP:

poor 1 2 3 4 5 6 7 8 9 10 excellent

RECORD

DATE ___/___/___ SLEPT FROM ___:___-___:___

LAST NIGHT I DREAMT . . .

REFLECT

I THINK THIS DREAM MEANS . . .

3 WORDS TO DESCRIBE MY DREAM:

COLORS IN MY DREAM:

- ☐ red
- ☐ pink
- ☐ black
- ☐ blue
- ☐ purple
- ☐ white
- ☐ yellow
- ☐ orange
- ☐ gray
- ☐ green
- ☐ brown
- ☐ other

WHAT DID I LEARN ABOUT MYSELF FROM THIS DREAM?

RATING MY STRESS THIS WEEK:

low 1 2 3 4 5 6 7 8 9 10 high

RECORD

DATE ___/___/___ SLEPT FROM ___:___-___:___

LAST NIGHT I DREAMT . . .

REFLECT

THINK THIS DREAM MEANS . . .

3 MAJOR THEMES IN MY DREAM:

MY NIGHTTIME ROUTINE INCLUDED:

- ☐ meditation
- ☐ self-care
- ☐ exercise
- ☐ social media
- ☐ friends/family
- ☐ alcohol
- ☐ reading
- ☐ work
- ☐ other

DID THIS DREAM REMIND ME OF ANYTHING IN MY PAST?

RATING MY MOOD WAKING UP:

poor 1 2 3 4 5 6 7 8 9 10 excellent

RECORD

DATE ___/___/___ SLEPT FROM ___:___-___:___

LAST NIGHT I DREAMT . . .

REFLECT

I THINK THIS DREAM MEANS . . .

3 SETTINGS IN MY DREAM:

NIGHTS I'VE HAD DREAMS THIS WEEK:

- ☐ Monday
- ☐ Tuesday
- ☐ Wednesday
- ☐ Thursday
- ☐ Friday
- ☐ Saturday
- ☐ Sunday

WHAT STOOD OUT MOST IN MY DREAM?

RATING MY ENJOYMENT OF MY DREAM:

poor 1 2 3 4 5 6 7 8 9 10 excellent

RECORD

DATE ___/___/___ SLEPT FROM ___:___-___:___

LAST NIGHT I DREAMT . . .

REFLECT

THINK THIS DREAM MEANS . . .

QUOTES FROM MY DREAM:

THIS DREAM REMINDED ME OF:

- ☐ childhood
- ☐ work
- ☐ friends
- ☐ relationships
- ☐ family
- ☐ other

HOW HAVE I BEEN FEELING OVER THE PAST FEW DAYS?

RATING HOW REALISTIC OR SURREAL MY DREAM FELT:

very realistic 1 2 3 4 5 6 7 8 9 10 very surreal

RECORD

DATE ___/___/___ SLEPT FROM ___:___-___:___

LAST NIGHT I DREAMT . . .

REFLECT

I THINK THIS DREAM MEANS . . .

3 SYMBOLS IN MY DREAM:

THIS DREAM TOOK PLACE:

- ☐ at home
- ☐ at work/school
- ☐ in nature
- ☐ in the city
- ☐ in an abstract place
- ☐ unknown
- ☐ other

WHAT WAS THE MOST UNUSUAL OR SURREAL PART OF MY DREAM?

RATING THE INTENSITY OF EMOTIONS (GOOD OR BAD) IN MY DREAM:

minimal 1 2 3 4 5 6 7 8 9 10 overwhelming

RECORD

DATE ___/___/___ SLEPT FROM ___:___-___:___

LAST NIGHT I DREAMT . . .

REFLECT

I THINK THIS DREAM MEANS . . .

THE DAY BEFORE MY DREAM CONSISTED OF:

- ☐ time outdoors
- ☐ work/school
- ☐ self-care
- ☐ time with friends/family
- ☐ chores
- ☐ downtime
- ☐ other

3 SIGNIFICANT COLORS IN MY DREAM:

WHAT KINDS OF DREAMS DO I WISH I HAD MORE OFTEN?

RATING THE CLARITY OF MY DREAM:

vague 1 2 3 4 5 6 7 8 9 10 extremely vivid

RECORD

DATE ___/___/___ SLEPT FROM ___:___-___:___

LAST NIGHT I DREAMT . . .

REFLECT

I THINK THIS DREAM MEANS . . .

THIS DREAM INCLUDED:

- ☐ people
- ☐ animals
- ☐ dialogue
- ☐ nature
- ☐ strong emotions
- ☐ fantasy elements
- ☐ other

3 SIGNIFICANT OBJECTS IN MY DREAM:

WHAT WAS THE MAIN EMOTION I FELT IN THIS DREAM?

RATING MY MOOD BEFORE BEDTIME:

poor 1 2 3 4 5 6 7 8 9 10 excellent

RECORD

DATE ___/___/___ SLEPT FROM ___:___-___:___

LAST NIGHT I DREAMT . . .

REFLECT

I THINK THIS DREAM MEANS . . .

3 POSSIBLE LESSONS FROM MY DREAM:

THIS DREAM INSPIRES ME TO:

- ☐ evaluate relationships
- ☐ take better care of myself
- ☐ advance my career
- ☐ improve sleep
- ☐ reduce stress
- ☐ other

WHAT PHYSICAL SENSATIONS DID I EXPERIENCE IN MY DREAM?

RATING MY WORK-LIFE BALANCE LATELY:

poor 1 2 3 4 5 6 7 8 9 10 excellent

RECORD

DATE ____/____/____ SLEPT FROM ____:____-____:____

LAST NIGHT I DREAMT . . .

REFLECT

I THINK THIS DREAM MEANS . . .

3 ACTIONS I TOOK IN MY DREAM:

THIS DREAM WAS:

- ☐ recurring
- ☐ surreal
- ☐ realistic
- ☐ enjoyable
- ☐ unpleasant
- ☐ long
- ☐ short
- ☐ other

DID MY DREAM HAVE A RESOLUTION OR DID IT FEEL UNFINISHED?

RATING THE SUPPORT SYSTEM CURRENTLY AROUND ME:

poor 1 2 3 4 5 6 7 8 9 10 excellent

RECORD

DATE ___/___/___ SLEPT FROM ___:___-___:___

LAST NIGHT I DREAMT . . .

REFLECT

THINK THIS DREAM MEANS . . .

3 PEOPLE WHO WERE IN MY DREAM:

THIS DREAM MADE ME FEEL:

- ☐ happy
- ☐ angry
- ☐ sad
- ☐ confused
- ☐ scared
- ☐ other

HOW DOES THIS DREAM RELATE TO MY LIFE?

RATING MY QUALITY OF SLEEP:

poor 1 2 3 4 5 6 7 8 9 10 excellent

RECORD

DATE ___/___/___ SLEPT FROM ___:___ ___:___

LAST NIGHT I DREAMT . . .

REFLECT

THINK THIS DREAM MEANS . . .

3 WORDS TO DESCRIBE MY DREAM:

COLORS IN MY DREAM:

- ☐ red
- ☐ pink
- ☐ black
- ☐ blue
- ☐ purple
- ☐ white
- ☐ yellow
- ☐ orange
- ☐ gray
- ☐ green
- ☐ brown
- ☐ other

WHAT DID I LEARN ABOUT MYSELF FROM THIS DREAM?

RATING MY STRESS THIS WEEK:

low 1 2 3 4 5 6 7 8 9 10 high

RECORD

DATE ___/___/___ SLEPT FROM ___.___-___:___

LAST NIGHT I DREAMT . . .

REFLECT

THINK THIS DREAM MEANS . . .

3 MAJOR THEMES IN MY DREAM:

MY NIGHTTIME ROUTINE INCLUDED:

- ☐ meditation
- ☐ self-care
- ☐ exercise
- ☐ social media
- ☐ friends/family
- ☐ alcohol
- ☐ reading
- ☐ work
- ☐ other

DID THIS DREAM REMIND ME OF ANYTHING IN MY PAST?

RATING MY MOOD WAKING UP:

poor 1 2 3 4 5 6 7 8 9 10 excellent

RECORD

DATE ___/___/___ SLEPT FROM ___:___-___:___

LAST NIGHT I DREAMT . . .

REFLECT

I THINK THIS DREAM MEANS . . .

NIGHTS I'VE HAD DREAMS THIS WEEK:

- ☐ Monday
- ☐ Tuesday
- ☐ Wednesday
- ☐ Thursday
- ☐ Friday
- ☐ Saturday
- ☐ Sunday

3 SETTINGS IN MY DREAM:

WHAT STOOD OUT MOST IN MY DREAM?

RATING MY ENJOYMENT OF MY DREAM:

poor 1 2 3 4 5 6 7 8 9 10 excellent

RECORD

DATE ___/___/___ SLEPT FROM ___:___ - ___:___

LAST NIGHT I DREAMT . . .

REFLECT

I THINK THIS DREAM MEANS . . .

3 QUOTES FROM MY DREAM:

THIS DREAM REMINDED ME OF:

- ☐ childhood
- ☐ work
- ☐ friends
- ☐ relationships
- ☐ family
- ☐ other

HOW HAVE I BEEN FEELING OVER THE PAST FEW DAYS?

RATING HOW REALISTIC OR SURREAL MY DREAM FELT:

very realistic 1 2 3 4 5 6 7 8 9 10 very surreal

RECORD

DATE ___/___/___ SLEPT FROM ___:___-___:___

LAST NIGHT I DREAMT . . .

REFLECT

I THINK THIS DREAM MEANS . . .

3 SYMBOLS IN MY DREAM:

THIS DREAM TOOK PLACE:

- ☐ at home
- ☐ at work/school
- ☐ in nature
- ☐ in the city
- ☐ in an abstract place
- ☐ unknown
- ☐ other

WHAT WAS THE MOST UNUSUAL OR SURREAL PART OF MY DREAM?

RATING THE INTENSITY OF EMOTIONS (GOOD OR BAD) IN MY DREAM:

minimal 1 2 3 4 5 6 7 8 9 10 overwhelming

RECORD

DATE ___/___/___ SLEPT FROM ___:___-___:___

LAST NIGHT I DREAMT . . .

REFLECT

I THINK THIS DREAM MEANS . . .

3 SIGNIFICANT COLORS IN MY DREAM:

THE DAY BEFORE MY DREAM CONSISTED OF:

- ☐ time outdoors
- ☐ work/school
- ☐ self-care
- ☐ time with friends/family
- ☐ chores
- ☐ downtime
- ☐ other

WHAT KINDS OF DREAMS DO I WISH I HAD MORE OFTEN?

RATING THE CLARITY OF MY DREAM:

vague 1 2 3 4 5 6 7 8 9 10 extremely vivid

RECORD

DATE ___/___/___ SLEPT FROM ___:___-___:___

LAST NIGHT I DREAMT . . .

REFLECT

I THINK THIS DREAM MEANS . . .

THIS DREAM INCLUDED:

- ☐ people
- ☐ animals
- ☐ dialogue
- ☐ nature
- ☐ strong emotions
- ☐ fantasy elements
- ☐ other

3 SIGNIFICANT OBJECTS IN MY DREAM:

WHAT WAS THE MAIN EMOTION I FELT IN THIS DREAM?

RATING MY MOOD BEFORE BEDTIME:

poor 1 2 3 4 5 6 7 8 9 10 excellent

RECORD

DATE ___/___/___ SLEPT FROM ___:___-___:___

LAST NIGHT I DREAMT . . .

REFLECT

I THINK THIS DREAM MEANS . . .

THIS DREAM INSPIRES ME TO:

- ☐ evaluate relationships
- ☐ take better care of myself
- ☐ advance my career
- ☐ improve sleep
- ☐ reduce stress
- ☐ other

3 POSSIBLE LESSONS FROM MY DREAM:

WHAT PHYSICAL SENSATIONS DID I EXPERIENCE IN MY DREAM?

RATING MY WORK-LIFE BALANCE LATELY:

poor 1 2 3 4 5 6 7 8 9 10 excellent

RECORD

DATE ___/___/___ SLEPT FROM ___:___-___:___

LAST NIGHT I DREAMT . . .

REFLECT

THINK THIS DREAM MEANS . . .

S ACTIONS I TOOK IN MY DREAM:

THIS DREAM WAS:

- ☐ recurring
- ☐ unpleasant
- ☐ surreal
- ☐ long
- ☐ realistic
- ☐ short
- ☐ enjoyable
- ☐ other

DID MY DREAM HAVE A RESOLUTION OR DID IT FEEL UNFINISHED?

RATING THE SUPPORT SYSTEM CURRENTLY AROUND ME:

poor 1 2 3 4 5 6 7 8 9 10 excellent

RECORD

DATE ___/___/___ SLEPT FROM ___:___ - ___:___

LAST NIGHT I DREAMT . . .

REFLECT

THINK THIS DREAM MEANS . . .

S PEOPLE WHO WERE IN MY DREAM:

THIS DREAM MADE ME FEEL:

- [ ] happy
- [ ] angry
- [ ] sad
- [ ] confused
- [ ] scared
- [ ] other

HOW DOES THIS DREAM RELATE TO MY LIFE?

RATING MY QUALITY OF SLEEP:

poor 1 2 3 4 5 6 7 8 9 10 excellent

RECORD

DATE ___/___/___ SLEPT FROM ___:___-___:___

LAST NIGHT I DREAMT . . .

REFLECT

I THINK THIS DREAM MEANS . . .

3 WORDS TO DESCRIBE MY DREAM:

COLORS IN MY DREAM:

- ☐ red
- ☐ pink
- ☐ black
- ☐ blue
- ☐ purple
- ☐ white
- ☐ yellow
- ☐ orange
- ☐ gray
- ☐ green
- ☐ brown
- ☐ other

WHAT DID I LEARN ABOUT MYSELF FROM THIS DREAM?

RATING MY STRESS THIS WEEK:

low 1 2 3 4 5 6 7 8 9 10 high

RECORD

DATE ___/___/___ SLEPT FROM ___:___-___:___

LAST NIGHT I DREAMT . . .

REFLECT

I THINK THIS DREAM MEANS . . .

3 MAJOR THEMES IN MY DREAM:

MY NIGHTTIME ROUTINE INCLUDED:

- ☐ meditation
- ☐ self-care
- ☐ exercise
- ☐ social media
- ☐ friends/family
- ☐ alcohol
- ☐ reading
- ☐ work
- ☐ other

DID THIS DREAM REMIND ME OF ANYTHING IN MY PAST?

RATING MY MOOD WAKING UP:

poor 1 2 3 4 5 6 7 8 9 10 excellent

RECORD

DATE ____/____/____ SLEPT FROM ____:____-____:____

LAST NIGHT I DREAMT . . .

REFLECT

I THINK THIS DREAM MEANS . . .

3 SETTINGS IN MY DREAM:

NIGHTS I'VE HAD DREAMS THIS WEEK:

☐ Monday ☐ Thursday ☐ Saturday
☐ Tuesday ☐ Friday ☐ Sunday
☐ Wednesday

WHAT STOOD OUT MOST IN MY DREAM?

RATING MY ENJOYMENT OF MY DREAM:

poor 1 2 3 4 5 6 7 8 9 10 excellent

RECORD

DATE ___/___/___ SLEPT FROM ___:___-___:___

LAST NIGHT I DREAMT . . .

REFLECT

I THINK THIS DREAM MEANS . . .

3 QUOTES FROM MY DREAM:

THIS DREAM REMINDED ME OF:

- ☐ childhood
- ☐ work
- ☐ friends
- ☐ relationships
- ☐ family
- ☐ other

HOW HAVE I BEEN FEELING OVER THE PAST FEW DAYS?

RATING HOW REALISTIC OR SURREAL MY DREAM FELT:

very realistic 1 2 3 4 5 6 7 8 9 10 very surreal

RECORD

DATE ___/___/___ SLEPT FROM ___:___-___:___

LAST NIGHT I DREAMT . . .

REFLECT

I THINK THIS DREAM MEANS . . .

3 SYMBOLS IN MY DREAM:

THIS DREAM TOOK PLACE:

- ☐ at home
- ☐ at work/school
- ☐ in nature
- ☐ in the city
- ☐ in an abstract place
- ☐ unknown
- ☐ other

WHAT WAS THE MOST UNUSUAL OR SURREAL PART OF MY DREAM?

RATING THE INTENSITY OF EMOTIONS (GOOD OR BAD) IN MY DREAM:

minimal 1 2 3 4 5 6 7 8 9 10 overwhelming

RECORD

DATE ___/___/___ SLEPT FROM ___:___-___:___

LAST NIGHT I DREAMT . . .

REFLECT

I THINK THIS DREAM MEANS . . .

THE DAY BEFORE MY DREAM CONSISTED OF:

- ☐ time outdoors
- ☐ work/school
- ☐ self-care
- ☐ time with friends/family
- ☐ chores
- ☐ downtime
- ☐ other

3 SIGNIFICANT COLORS IN MY DREAM:

WHAT KINDS OF DREAMS DO I WISH I HAD MORE OFTEN?

RATING THE CLARITY OF MY DREAM:

vague 1 2 3 4 5 6 7 8 9 10 extremely vivid

RECORD

DATE ___/___/___ SLEPT FROM ___:___-___:___

LAST NIGHT I DREAMT . . .

REFLECT

THINK THIS DREAM MEANS . . .

THIS DREAM INCLUDED:

- ☐ people
- ☐ animals
- ☐ dialogue
- ☐ nature
- ☐ strong emotions
- ☐ fantasy elements
- ☐ other

3 SIGNIFICANT OBJECTS IN MY DREAM:

WHAT WAS THE MAIN EMOTION I FELT IN THIS DREAM?

RATING MY MOOD BEFORE BEDTIME:

poor 1 2 3 4 5 6 7 8 9 10 excellent

RECORD

DATE ___/___/___ SLEPT FROM ___:___-___:___

LAST NIGHT I DREAMT . . .

REFLECT

I THINK THIS DREAM MEANS . . .

THIS DREAM INSPIRES ME TO:

- ☐ evaluate relationships
- ☐ take better care of myself
- ☐ advance my career
- ☐ improve sleep
- ☐ reduce stress
- ☐ other

POSSIBLE LESSONS FROM MY DREAM:

WHAT PHYSICAL SENSATIONS DID I EXPERIENCE IN MY DREAM?

RATING MY WORK-LIFE BALANCE LATELY:

poor 1 2 3 4 5 6 7 8 9 10 excellent

RECORD

DATE ___/___/___ SLEPT FROM ___:___-___:___

LAST NIGHT I DREAMT . . .

REFLECT

I THINK THIS DREAM MEANS . . .

3 ACTIONS I TOOK IN MY DREAM:

THIS DREAM WAS:

- ☐ recurring
- ☐ surreal
- ☐ realistic
- ☐ enjoyable
- ☐ unpleasant
- ☐ long
- ☐ short
- ☐ other

DID MY DREAM HAVE A RESOLUTION OR DID IT FEEL UNFINISHED?

RATING THE SUPPORT SYSTEM CURRENTLY AROUND ME:

poor 1 2 3 4 5 6 7 8 9 10 excellent

RECORD

DATE ___/___/___ SLEPT FROM ___:___ - ___:___

LAST NIGHT I DREAMT . . .

REFLECT

I THINK THIS DREAM MEANS . . .

3 PEOPLE WHO WERE IN MY DREAM:

THIS DREAM MADE ME FEEL:

- ☐ happy
- ☐ angry
- ☐ sad
- ☐ confused
- ☐ scared
- ☐ other

HOW DOES THIS DREAM RELATE TO MY LIFE?

RATING MY QUALITY OF SLEEP:

poor 1 2 3 4 5 6 7 8 9 10 excellent

RECORD

DATE ___/___/___ SLEPT FROM ___:___-___:___

LAST NIGHT I DREAMT . . .

REFLECT

I THINK THIS DREAM MEANS . . .

3 WORDS TO DESCRIBE MY DREAM:

COLORS IN MY DREAM:

- ☐ red
- ☐ pink
- ☐ black
- ☐ blue
- ☐ purple
- ☐ white
- ☐ yellow
- ☐ orange
- ☐ gray
- ☐ green
- ☐ brown
- ☐ other

WHAT DID I LEARN ABOUT MYSELF FROM THIS DREAM?

RATING MY STRESS THIS WEEK:

low 1 2 3 4 5 6 7 8 9 10 high

RECORD

DATE ___/___/___ SLEPT FROM ___:___-___:___

LAST NIGHT I DREAMT . . .

REFLECT

I THINK THIS DREAM MEANS . . .

3 MAJOR THEMES IN MY DREAM:

MY NIGHTTIME ROUTINE INCLUDED:

- ☐ meditation
- ☐ self-care
- ☐ exercise
- ☐ social media
- ☐ friends/family
- ☐ alcohol
- ☐ reading
- ☐ work
- ☐ other

DID THIS DREAM REMIND ME OF ANYTHING IN MY PAST?

RATING MY MOOD WAKING UP:

poor 1 2 3 4 5 6 7 8 9 10 excellent

RECORD

DATE ____/____/____ SLEPT FROM ____:____-____:____

LAST NIGHT I DREAMT . . .

REFLECT

THINK THIS DREAM MEANS . . .

3 SETTINGS IN MY DREAM:

NIGHTS I'VE HAD DREAMS THIS WEEK:

- ☐ Monday
- ☐ Tuesday
- ☐ Wednesday
- ☐ Thursday
- ☐ Friday
- ☐ Saturday
- ☐ Sunday

WHAT STOOD OUT MOST IN MY DREAM?

RATING MY ENJOYMENT OF MY DREAM:

poor 1 2 3 4 5 6 7 8 9 10 excellent

RECORD

DATE ___/___/___ SLEPT FROM ___:___-___:___

LAST NIGHT I DREAMT . . .

REFLECT

I THINK THIS DREAM MEANS . . .

3 QUOTES FROM MY DREAM:

THIS DREAM REMINDED ME OF:

- ☐ childhood
- ☐ work
- ☐ friends
- ☐ relationships
- ☐ family
- ☐ other

HOW HAVE I BEEN FEELING OVER THE PAST FEW DAYS?

RATING HOW REALISTIC OR SURREAL MY DREAM FELT:

very realistic 1 2 3 4 5 6 7 8 9 10 very surreal

RECORD

DATE ___/___/___ SLEPT FROM ___:___ - ___:___

LAST NIGHT I DREAMT . . .

REFLECT

THINK THIS DREAM MEANS . . .

3 SYMBOLS IN MY DREAM:

THIS DREAM TOOK PLACE:

- ☐ at home
- ☐ at work/school
- ☐ in nature
- ☐ in the city
- ☐ in an abstract place
- ☐ unknown
- ☐ other

WHAT WAS THE MOST UNUSUAL OR SURREAL PART OF MY DREAM?

RATING THE INTENSITY OF EMOTIONS (GOOD OR BAD) IN MY DREAM:

minimal 1 2 3 4 5 6 7 8 9 10 overwhelming

RECORD

DATE ___/___/___ SLEPT FROM ___:___-___:___

LAST NIGHT I DREAMT . . .

REFLECT

THINK THIS DREAM MEANS . . .

THE DAY BEFORE MY DREAM CONSISTED OF:

- ☐ time outdoors
- ☐ work/school
- ☐ self-care
- ☐ time with friends/family
- ☐ chores
- ☐ downtime
- ☐ other

3 SIGNIFICANT COLORS IN MY DREAM:

WHAT KINDS OF DREAMS DO I WISH I HAD MORE OFTEN?

RATING THE CLARITY OF MY DREAM:

vague 1 2 3 4 5 6 7 8 9 10 extremely vivid

RECORD

DATE ___/___/___ SLEPT FROM ___:___-___:___

LAST NIGHT I DREAMT . . .

REFLECT

I THINK THIS DREAM MEANS . . .

THIS DREAM INCLUDED:

- ☐ people
- ☐ animals
- ☐ dialogue
- ☐ nature
- ☐ strong emotions
- ☐ fantasy elements
- ☐ other

3 SIGNIFICANT OBJECTS IN MY DREAM:

WHAT WAS THE MAIN EMOTION I FELT IN THIS DREAM?

RATING MY MOOD BEFORE BEDTIME:

poor 1 2 3 4 5 6 7 8 9 10 excellent

RECORD

DATE ___/___/___ SLEPT FROM ___:___-___:___

LAST NIGHT I DREAMT . . .

REFLECT

I THINK THIS DREAM MEANS . . .

THIS DREAM INSPIRES ME TO:

- ☐ evaluate relationships
- ☐ take better care of myself
- ☐ advance my career
- ☐ improve sleep
- ☐ reduce stress
- ☐ other

3 POSSIBLE LESSONS FROM MY DREAM:

WHAT PHYSICAL SENSATIONS DID I EXPERIENCE IN MY DREAM?

RATING MY WORK-LIFE BALANCE LATELY:

poor 1 2 3 4 5 6 7 8 9 10 excellent

RECORD

DATE ___/___/___ SLEPT FROM ___:___-___:___

LAST NIGHT I DREAMT . . .

REFLECT

I THINK THIS DREAM MEANS . . .

3 ACTIONS I TOOK IN MY DREAM:

THIS DREAM WAS:

- ☐ recurring
- ☐ surreal
- ☐ realistic
- ☐ enjoyable
- ☐ unpleasant
- ☐ long
- ☐ short
- ☐ other

DID MY DREAM HAVE A RESOLUTION OR DID IT FEEL UNFINISHED?

RATING THE SUPPORT SYSTEM CURRENTLY AROUND ME:

poor 1 2 3 4 5 6 7 8 9 10 excellent

RECORD

DATE ___/___/___ SLEPT FROM ___:___-___:___

LAST NIGHT I DREAMT . . .

REFLECT

I THINK THIS DREAM MEANS . . .

3 PEOPLE WHO WERE IN MY DREAM:

THIS DREAM MADE ME FEEL:

- ☐ happy
- ☐ angry
- ☐ sad
- ☐ confused
- ☐ scared
- ☐ other

HOW DOES THIS DREAM RELATE TO MY LIFE?

RATING MY QUALITY OF SLEEP:

poor 1 2 3 4 5 6 7 8 9 10 excellent

RECORD

DATE ___/___/___ SLEPT FROM ___:___-___:___

LAST NIGHT I DREAMT . . .

REFLECT

I THINK THIS DREAM MEANS . . .

3 WORDS TO DESCRIBE MY DREAM:

COLORS IN MY DREAM:

- ☐ red
- ☐ pink
- ☐ black
- ☐ blue
- ☐ purple
- ☐ white
- ☐ yellow
- ☐ orange
- ☐ gray
- ☐ green
- ☐ brown
- ☐ other

WHAT DID I LEARN ABOUT MYSELF FROM THIS DREAM?

RATING MY STRESS THIS WEEK:

low 1 2 3 4 5 6 7 8 9 10 high

RECORD

DATE ___/___/___ SLEPT FROM ___:___-___:___

LAST NIGHT I DREAMT . . .

REFLECT

I THINK THIS DREAM MEANS . . .

3 MAJOR THEMES IN MY DREAM:

MY NIGHTTIME ROUTINE INCLUDED:

- ☐ meditation
- ☐ self-care
- ☐ exercise
- ☐ social media
- ☐ friends/family
- ☐ alcohol
- ☐ reading
- ☐ work
- ☐ other

DID THIS DREAM REMIND ME OF ANYTHING IN MY PAST?

RATING MY MOOD WAKING UP:

poor 1 2 3 4 5 6 7 8 9 10 excellent

RECORD

DATE ___/___/___ SLEPT FROM ___:___-___:___

LAST NIGHT I DREAMT . . .

REFLECT

THINK THIS DREAM MEANS . . .

3 SETTINGS IN MY DREAM:

NIGHTS I'VE HAD DREAMS THIS WEEK:

- ☐ Monday
- ☐ Tuesday
- ☐ Wednesday
- ☐ Thursday
- ☐ Friday
- ☐ Saturday
- ☐ Sunday

WHAT STOOD OUT MOST IN MY DREAM?

RATING MY ENJOYMENT OF MY DREAM:

poor 1 2 3 4 5 6 7 8 9 10 excellent

RECORD

DATE ___/___/___ SLEPT FROM ___:___-___:___

LAST NIGHT I DREAMT . . .

REFLECT

THINK THIS DREAM MEANS . . .

QUOTES FROM MY DREAM:

THIS DREAM REMINDED ME OF:

- [ ] childhood
- [ ] work
- [ ] friends
- [ ] relationships
- [ ] family
- [ ] other

OW HAVE I BEEN FEELING OVER THE PAST FEW DAYS?

RATING HOW REALISTIC OR SURREAL MY DREAM FELT:

very realistic 1 2 3 4 5 6 7 8 9 10 very surreal

RECORD

DATE ___/___/___ SLEPT FROM ___:___-___:___

LAST NIGHT I DREAMT . . .

REFLECT

THINK THIS DREAM MEANS . . .

3 SYMBOLS IN MY DREAM:

THIS DREAM TOOK PLACE:

- ☐ at home
- ☐ at work/school
- ☐ in nature
- ☐ in the city
- ☐ in an abstract place
- ☐ unknown
- ☐ other

WHAT WAS THE MOST UNUSUAL OR SURREAL PART OF MY DREAM?

RATING THE INTENSITY OF EMOTIONS (GOOD OR BAD) IN MY DREAM:

minimal 1 2 3 4 5 6 7 8 9 10 overwhelming

RECORD

DATE ___/___/___ SLEPT FROM ___:___ - ___:___

LAST NIGHT I DREAMT . . .

REFLECT

I THINK THIS DREAM MEANS . . .

THE DAY BEFORE MY DREAM CONSISTED OF:

- ☐ time outdoors
- ☐ work/school
- ☐ self-care
- ☐ time with friends/family
- ☐ chores
- ☐ downtime
- ☐ other

3 SIGNIFICANT COLORS IN MY DREAM:

WHAT KINDS OF DREAMS DO I WISH I HAD MORE OFTEN?

RATING THE CLARITY OF MY DREAM:

vague 1 2 3 4 5 6 7 8 9 10 extremely vivid

RECORD

DATE ___/___/___ SLEPT FROM ___:___-___:___

LAST NIGHT I DREAMT . . .

REFLECT

I THINK THIS DREAM MEANS . . .

THIS DREAM INCLUDED:

- ☐ people
- ☐ animals
- ☐ dialogue
- ☐ nature
- ☐ strong emotions
- ☐ fantasy elements
- ☐ other

3 SIGNIFICANT OBJECTS IN MY DREAM:

WHAT WAS THE MAIN EMOTION I FELT IN THIS DREAM?

RATING MY MOOD BEFORE BEDTIME:

poor 1 2 3 4 5 6 7 8 9 10 excellent

RECORD

DATE ___/___/___ SLEPT FROM ___:___-___:___

LAST NIGHT I DREAMT . . .

REFLECT

I THINK THIS DREAM MEANS . . .

THIS DREAM INSPIRES ME TO:

- ☐ evaluate relationships
- ☐ take better care of myself
- ☐ advance my career
- ☐ improve sleep
- ☐ reduce stress
- ☐ other

3 POSSIBLE LESSONS FROM MY DREAM:

WHAT PHYSICAL SENSATIONS DID I EXPERIENCE IN MY DREAM?

RATING MY WORK-LIFE BALANCE LATELY:

poor 1 2 3 4 5 6 7 8 9 10 excellent

RECORD

DATE ___/___/___ SLEPT FROM ___:___-___:___

LAST NIGHT I DREAMT . . .

REFLECT

I THINK THIS DREAM MEANS . . .

3 ACTIONS I TOOK IN MY DREAM:

THIS DREAM WAS:

- ☐ recurring
- ☐ surreal
- ☐ realistic
- ☐ enjoyable
- ☐ unpleasant
- ☐ long
- ☐ short
- ☐ other

DID MY DREAM HAVE A RESOLUTION OR DID IT FEEL UNFINISHED?

RATING THE SUPPORT SYSTEM CURRENTLY AROUND ME:

poor 1 2 3 4 5 6 7 8 9 10 excellent

RECORD

DATE ___/___/___ SLEPT FROM ___:___ - ___:___

LAST NIGHT I DREAMT . . .

REFLECT

THINK THIS DREAM MEANS . . .

3 PEOPLE WHO WERE IN MY DREAM:

THIS DREAM MADE ME FEEL:

- ☐ happy
- ☐ angry
- ☐ sad
- ☐ confused
- ☐ scared
- ☐ other

HOW DOES THIS DREAM RELATE TO MY LIFE?

RATING MY QUALITY OF SLEEP:

poor 1 2 3 4 5 6 7 8 9 10 excellent

RECORD

DATE ___/___/___ SLEPT FROM ___:___-___:___

LAST NIGHT I DREAMT . . .

REFLECT

I THINK THIS DREAM MEANS . . .

3 WORDS TO DESCRIBE MY DREAM:

COLORS IN MY DREAM:

- ☐ red
- ☐ pink
- ☐ black
- ☐ blue
- ☐ purple
- ☐ white
- ☐ yellow
- ☐ orange
- ☐ gray
- ☐ green
- ☐ brown
- ☐ other

WHAT DID I LEARN ABOUT MYSELF FROM THIS DREAM?

RATING MY STRESS THIS WEEK:

low 1 2 3 4 5 6 7 8 9 10 high

RECORD

DATE ___/___/___ SLEPT FROM ___:___-___:___

LAST NIGHT I DREAMT . . .

REFLECT

THINK THIS DREAM MEANS . . .

3 MAJOR THEMES IN MY DREAM:

MY NIGHTTIME ROUTINE INCLUDED:

- ☐ meditation
- ☐ self-care
- ☐ exercise
- ☐ social media
- ☐ friends/family
- ☐ alcohol
- ☐ reading
- ☐ work
- ☐ other

DID THIS DREAM REMIND ME OF ANYTHING IN MY PAST?

RATING MY MOOD WAKING UP:

poor 1 2 3 4 5 6 7 8 9 10 excellent

RECORD

DATE ___/___/___ SLEPT FROM ___:___ - ___:___

LAST NIGHT I DREAMT . . .

REFLECT

I THINK THIS DREAM MEANS . . .

3 SETTINGS IN MY DREAM:

NIGHTS I'VE HAD DREAMS THIS WEEK:

- ☐ Monday
- ☐ Tuesday
- ☐ Wednesday
- ☐ Thursday
- ☐ Friday
- ☐ Saturday
- ☐ Sunday

WHAT STOOD OUT MOST IN MY DREAM?

RATING MY ENJOYMENT OF MY DREAM:

poor 1 2 3 4 5 6 7 8 9 10 excellent

RECORD

DATE ___/___/___ SLEPT FROM ___:___-___:___

LAST NIGHT I DREAMT . . .

REFLECT

I THINK THIS DREAM MEANS . . .

3 QUOTES FROM MY DREAM:

THIS DREAM REMINDED ME OF:

- ☐ childhood
- ☐ work
- ☐ friends
- ☐ relationships
- ☐ family
- ☐ other

HOW HAVE I BEEN FEELING OVER THE PAST FEW DAYS?

RATING HOW REALISTIC OR SURREAL MY DREAM FELT:

very realistic 1 2 3 4 5 6 7 8 9 10 very surreal

RECORD

DATE ___/___/___ SLEPT FROM ___:___-___:___

LAST NIGHT I DREAMT . . .

REFLECT

I THINK THIS DREAM MEANS . . .

3 SYMBOLS IN MY DREAM:

THIS DREAM TOOK PLACE:

- ☐ at home
- ☐ at work/school
- ☐ in nature
- ☐ in the city
- ☐ in an abstract place
- ☐ unknown
- ☐ other

WHAT WAS THE MOST UNUSUAL OR SURREAL PART OF MY DREAM?

RATING THE INTENSITY OF EMOTIONS (GOOD OR BAD) IN MY DREAM:

minimal 1 2 3 4 5 6 7 8 9 10 overwhelming

RECORD

DATE ___/___/___ SLEPT FROM ___:___-___:___

LAST NIGHT I DREAMT . . .

REFLECT

I THINK THIS DREAM MEANS . . .

THE DAY BEFORE MY DREAM CONSISTED OF:

- ☐ time outdoors
- ☐ work/school
- ☐ self-care
- ☐ time with friends/family
- ☐ chores
- ☐ downtime
- ☐ other

3 SIGNIFICANT COLORS IN MY DREAM:

WHAT KINDS OF DREAMS DO I WISH I HAD MORE OFTEN?

RATING THE CLARITY OF MY DREAM:

vague 1 2 3 4 5 6 7 8 9 10 extremely vivid

RECORD

DATE ___/___/___ SLEPT FROM ___:___-___:___

LAST NIGHT I DREAMT . . .

REFLECT

I THINK THIS DREAM MEANS . . .

3 SIGNIFICANT OBJECTS IN MY DREAM:

THIS DREAM INCLUDED:

- ☐ people
- ☐ animals
- ☐ dialogue
- ☐ nature
- ☐ strong emotions
- ☐ fantasy elements
- ☐ other

WHAT WAS THE MAIN EMOTION I FELT IN THIS DREAM?

RATING MY MOOD BEFORE BEDTIME:

poor 1 2 3 4 5 6 7 8 9 10 excellent

RECORD

DATE ___/___/___ SLEPT FROM ___:___-___:___

LAST NIGHT I DREAMT . . .

REFLECT

I THINK THIS DREAM MEANS . . .

3 POSSIBLE LESSONS FROM MY DREAM:

THIS DREAM INSPIRES ME TO:

- ☐ evaluate relationships
- ☐ take better care of myself
- ☐ advance my career
- ☐ improve sleep
- ☐ reduce stress
- ☐ other

WHAT PHYSICAL SENSATIONS DID I EXPERIENCE IN MY DREAM?

RATING MY WORK-LIFE BALANCE LATELY:

poor 1 2 3 4 5 6 7 8 9 10 excellent

RECORD

DATE ___/___/___ SLEPT FROM ___:___-___:___

LAST NIGHT I DREAMT . . .

REFLECT

THINK THIS DREAM MEANS . . .

ACTIONS I TOOK IN MY DREAM:

THIS DREAM WAS:

- ☐ recurring
- ☐ surreal
- ☐ realistic
- ☐ enjoyable
- ☐ unpleasant
- ☐ long
- ☐ short
- ☐ other

DID MY DREAM HAVE A RESOLUTION OR DID IT FEEL UNFINISHED?

RATING THE SUPPORT SYSTEM CURRENTLY AROUND ME:

poor 1 2 3 4 5 6 7 8 9 10 excellent

RECORD

DATE ___/___/___ SLEPT FROM ___:___-___:___

LAST NIGHT I DREAMT . . .

REFLECT

THINK THIS DREAM MEANS . . .

S PEOPLE WHO WERE IN MY DREAM:

THIS DREAM MADE ME FEEL:

- [ ] happy
- [ ] angry
- [ ] sad
- [ ] confused
- [ ] scared
- [ ] other

HOW DOES THIS DREAM RELATE TO MY LIFE?

RATING MY QUALITY OF SLEEP:

poor 1 2 3 4 5 6 7 8 9 10 excellent

RECORD

DATE ___/___/___ SLEPT FROM ___:___ - ___:___

LAST NIGHT I DREAMT . . .

REFLECT

THINK THIS DREAM MEANS . . .

3 WORDS TO DESCRIBE MY DREAM:

COLORS IN MY DREAM:

- ☐ red
- ☐ pink
- ☐ black
- ☐ blue
- ☐ purple
- ☐ white
- ☐ yellow
- ☐ orange
- ☐ gray
- ☐ green
- ☐ brown
- ☐ other

WHAT DID I LEARN ABOUT MYSELF FROM THIS DREAM?

RATING MY STRESS THIS WEEK:

low 1 2 3 4 5 6 7 8 9 10 high

RECORD

DATE ___/___/___ SLEPT FROM ___:___-___:___

LAST NIGHT I DREAMT . . .

REFLECT

I THINK THIS DREAM MEANS . . .

3 MAJOR THEMES IN MY DREAM:

MY NIGHTTIME ROUTINE INCLUDED:

- ☐ meditation
- ☐ self-care
- ☐ exercise
- ☐ social media
- ☐ friends/family
- ☐ alcohol
- ☐ reading
- ☐ work
- ☐ other

DID THIS DREAM REMIND ME OF ANYTHING IN MY PAST?

RATING MY MOOD WAKING UP:

poor 1 2 3 4 5 6 7 8 9 10 excellent

RECORD

DATE ___/___/___ SLEPT FROM ___:___-___:___

LAST NIGHT I DREAMT . . .

REFLECT

I THINK THIS DREAM MEANS . . .

3 SETTINGS IN MY DREAM:

NIGHTS I'VE HAD DREAMS THIS WEEK:

- ☐ Monday
- ☐ Tuesday
- ☐ Wednesday
- ☐ Thursday
- ☐ Friday
- ☐ Saturday
- ☐ Sunday

WHAT STOOD OUT MOST IN MY DREAM?

RATING MY ENJOYMENT OF MY DREAM:

poor 1 2 3 4 5 6 7 8 9 10 excellent

RECORD

DATE ___/___/___ SLEPT FROM ___:___-___:___

LAST NIGHT I DREAMT . . .

REFLECT

I THINK THIS DREAM MEANS . . .

3 QUOTES FROM MY DREAM:

THIS DREAM REMINDED ME OF:

- ☐ childhood
- ☐ work
- ☐ friends
- ☐ relationships
- ☐ family
- ☐ other

HOW HAVE I BEEN FEELING OVER THE PAST FEW DAYS?

RATING HOW REALISTIC OR SURREAL MY DREAM FELT:

very realistic 1 2 3 4 5 6 7 8 9 10 very surreal

RECORD

DATE ___/___/___ SLEPT FROM ___:___-___:___

LAST NIGHT I DREAMT . . .

REFLECT

I THINK THIS DREAM MEANS . . .

3 SYMBOLS IN MY DREAM:

THIS DREAM TOOK PLACE:

- ☐ at home
- ☐ at work/school
- ☐ in nature
- ☐ in the city
- ☐ in an abstract place
- ☐ unknown
- ☐ other

WHAT WAS THE MOST UNUSUAL OR SURREAL PART OF MY DREAM?

RATING THE INTENSITY OF EMOTIONS (GOOD OR BAD) IN MY DREAM:

minimal 1 2 3 4 5 6 7 8 9 10 overwhelming

RECORD

DATE ____/____/____ SLEPT FROM ____:____-____:____

LAST NIGHT I DREAMT . . .

REFLECT

I THINK THIS DREAM MEANS . . .

THE DAY BEFORE MY DREAM CONSISTED OF:

- ☐ time outdoors
- ☐ work/school
- ☐ self-care
- ☐ time with friends/family
- ☐ chores
- ☐ downtime
- ☐ other

SIGNIFICANT COLORS IN MY DREAM:

WHAT KINDS OF DREAMS DO I WISH I HAD MORE OFTEN?

RATING THE CLARITY OF MY DREAM:

vague 1 2 3 4 5 6 7 8 9 10 extremely vivid

RECORD

DATE ___/___/___ SLEPT FROM ___:___-___:___

LAST NIGHT I DREAMT . . .

REFLECT

THINK THIS DREAM MEANS . . .

THIS DREAM INCLUDED:

- ☐ people
- ☐ animals
- ☐ dialogue
- ☐ nature
- ☐ strong emotions
- ☐ fantasy elements
- ☐ other

SIGNIFICANT OBJECTS IN MY DREAM:

WHAT WAS THE MAIN EMOTION I FELT IN THIS DREAM?

RATING MY MOOD BEFORE BEDTIME:

poor 1 2 3 4 5 6 7 8 9 10 excellent

RECORD

DATE ___/___/___ SLEPT FROM ___:___-___:___

LAST NIGHT I DREAMT . . .

REFLECT

I THINK THIS DREAM MEANS . . .

3 POSSIBLE LESSONS FROM MY DREAM:

THIS DREAM INSPIRES ME TO:

- ☐ evaluate relationships
- ☐ take better care of myself
- ☐ advance my career
- ☐ improve sleep
- ☐ reduce stress
- ☐ other

WHAT PHYSICAL SENSATIONS DID I EXPERIENCE IN MY DREAM?

RATING MY WORK-LIFE BALANCE LATELY:

poor 1 2 3 4 5 6 7 8 9 10 excellent

RECORD

DATE ___/___/___ SLEPT FROM ___:___-___:___

LAST NIGHT I DREAMT . . .

REFLECT

I THINK THIS DREAM MEANS . . .

3 ACTIONS I TOOK IN MY DREAM:

THIS DREAM WAS:

- ☐ recurring
- ☐ surreal
- ☐ realistic
- ☐ enjoyable
- ☐ unpleasant
- ☐ long
- ☐ short
- ☐ other

DID MY DREAM HAVE A RESOLUTION OR DID IT FEEL UNFINISHED?

RATING THE SUPPORT SYSTEM CURRENTLY AROUND ME:

poor 1 2 3 4 5 6 7 8 9 10 excellent

RECORD

DATE ___/___/___ SLEPT FROM ___:___-___:___

LAST NIGHT I DREAMT . . .

REFLECT

I THINK THIS DREAM MEANS . . .

3 PEOPLE WHO WERE IN MY DREAM:

THIS DREAM MADE ME FEEL:

- ☐ happy
- ☐ angry
- ☐ sad
- ☐ confused
- ☐ scared
- ☐ other

HOW DOES THIS DREAM RELATE TO MY LIFE?

RATING MY QUALITY OF SLEEP:

poor 1 2 3 4 5 6 7 8 9 10 excellent

RECORD

DATE ___/___/___ SLEPT FROM ___:___-___:___

LAST NIGHT I DREAMT . . .

REFLECT

I THINK THIS DREAM MEANS . . .

3 WORDS TO DESCRIBE MY DREAM:

COLORS IN MY DREAM:

- ☐ red
- ☐ pink
- ☐ black
- ☐ blue
- ☐ purple
- ☐ white
- ☐ yellow
- ☐ orange
- ☐ gray
- ☐ green
- ☐ brown
- ☐ other

WHAT DID I LEARN ABOUT MYSELF FROM THIS DREAM?

RATING MY STRESS THIS WEEK:

low 1 2 3 4 5 6 7 8 9 10 high

RECORD

DATE ___/___/___ SLEPT FROM ___:___-___:___

LAST NIGHT I DREAMT . . .

REFLECT

I THINK THIS DREAM MEANS . . .

3 MAJOR THEMES IN MY DREAM:

MY NIGHTTIME ROUTINE INCLUDED:

- ☐ meditation
- ☐ self-care
- ☐ exercise
- ☐ social media
- ☐ friends/family
- ☐ alcohol
- ☐ reading
- ☐ work
- ☐ other

DID THIS DREAM REMIND ME OF ANYTHING IN MY PAST?

RATING MY MOOD WAKING UP:

poor 1 2 3 4 5 6 7 8 9 10 excellent

RECORD

DATE ___/___/___ SLEPT FROM ___:___-___:___

LAST NIGHT I DREAMT . . .

REFLECT

I THINK THIS DREAM MEANS . . .

3 SETTINGS IN MY DREAM:

NIGHTS I'VE HAD DREAMS THIS WEEK:

- ☐ Monday
- ☐ Tuesday
- ☐ Wednesday
- ☐ Thursday
- ☐ Friday
- ☐ Saturday
- ☐ Sunday

WHAT STOOD OUT MOST IN MY DREAM?

RATING MY ENJOYMENT OF MY DREAM:

poor 1 2 3 4 5 6 7 8 9 10 excellent

RECORD

DATE ___/___/___ SLEPT FROM ___:___-___:___

LAST NIGHT I DREAMT . . .

REFLECT

THINK THIS DREAM MEANS . . .

3 QUOTES FROM MY DREAM:

THIS DREAM REMINDED ME OF:

- [ ] childhood
- [ ] work
- [ ] friends
- [ ] relationships
- [ ] family
- [ ] other

HOW HAVE I BEEN FEELING OVER THE PAST FEW DAYS?

RATING HOW REALISTIC OR SURREAL MY DREAM FELT:

very realistic 1 2 3 4 5 6 7 8 9 10 very surreal

RECORD

DATE ___/___/___ SLEPT FROM ___:___-___:___

LAST NIGHT I DREAMT . . .

REFLECT

THINK THIS DREAM MEANS . . .

SYMBOLS IN MY DREAM:

THIS DREAM TOOK PLACE:

- ☐ at home
- ☐ at work/school
- ☐ in nature
- ☐ in the city
- ☐ in an abstract place
- ☐ unknown
- ☐ other

WHAT WAS THE MOST UNUSUAL OR SURREAL PART OF MY DREAM?

RATING THE INTENSITY OF EMOTIONS (GOOD OR BAD) IN MY DREAM:

minimal 1 2 3 4 5 6 7 8 9 10 overwhelming

RECORD

DATE ___/___/___ SLEPT FROM ___:___-___:___

LAST NIGHT I DREAMT . . .

REFLECT

I THINK THIS DREAM MEANS . . .

SIGNIFICANT COLORS IN MY DREAM:

THE DAY BEFORE MY DREAM CONSISTED OF:

- ☐ time outdoors
- ☐ work/school
- ☐ self-care
- ☐ time with friends/family
- ☐ chores
- ☐ downtime
- ☐ other

WHAT KINDS OF DREAMS DO I WISH I HAD MORE OFTEN?

RATING THE CLARITY OF MY DREAM:

vague 1 2 3 4 5 6 7 8 9 10 extremely vivid

RECORD

DATE ___/___/___ SLEPT FROM ___:___-___:___

LAST NIGHT I DREAMT . . .

REFLECT

THINK THIS DREAM MEANS . . .

THIS DREAM INCLUDED:

- ☐ people
- ☐ animals
- ☐ dialogue
- ☐ nature
- ☐ strong emotions
- ☐ fantasy elements
- ☐ other

SIGNIFICANT OBJECTS IN MY DREAM:

WHAT WAS THE MAIN EMOTION I FELT IN THIS DREAM?

RATING MY MOOD BEFORE BEDTIME:

poor 1 2 3 4 5 6 7 8 9 10 excellent

RECORD

DATE ___/___/___ SLEPT FROM ___:___-___:___

LAST NIGHT I DREAMT . . .

REFLECT

I THINK THIS DREAM MEANS . . .

THIS DREAM INSPIRES ME TO:

- ☐ evaluate relationships
- ☐ take better care of myself
- ☐ advance my career
- ☐ improve sleep
- ☐ reduce stress
- ☐ other

3 POSSIBLE LESSONS FROM MY DREAM:

WHAT PHYSICAL SENSATIONS DID I EXPERIENCE IN MY DREAM?

RATING MY WORK-LIFE BALANCE LATELY:

poor 1 2 3 4 5 6 7 8 9 10 excellent

RECORD

DATE ___/___/___ SLEPT FROM ___:___-___:___

LAST NIGHT I DREAMT . . .

REFLECT

I THINK THIS DREAM MEANS . . .

3 ACTIONS I TOOK IN MY DREAM:

THIS DREAM WAS:

- ☐ recurring
- ☐ surreal
- ☐ realistic
- ☐ enjoyable
- ☐ unpleasant
- ☐ long
- ☐ short
- ☐ other

DID MY DREAM HAVE A RESOLUTION OR DID IT FEEL UNFINISHED?

RATING THE SUPPORT SYSTEM CURRENTLY AROUND ME:

poor 1 2 3 4 5 6 7 8 9 10 excellent

RECORD

DATE ___/___/___ SLEPT FROM ___:___-___:___

LAST NIGHT I DREAMT . . .

REFLECT

I THINK THIS DREAM MEANS . . .

3 PEOPLE WHO WERE IN MY DREAM:

THIS DREAM MADE ME FEEL:

- ☐ happy
- ☐ angry
- ☐ sad
- ☐ confused
- ☐ scared
- ☐ other

HOW DOES THIS DREAM RELATE TO MY LIFE?

RATING MY QUALITY OF SLEEP:

poor 1 2 3 4 5 6 7 8 9 10 excellent

RECORD

DATE ____/____/____ SLEPT FROM ____:____-____:____

LAST NIGHT I DREAMT . . .

REFLECT

I THINK THIS DREAM MEANS . . .

3 WORDS TO DESCRIBE MY DREAM:

COLORS IN MY DREAM:

- ☐ red
- ☐ pink
- ☐ black
- ☐ blue
- ☐ purple
- ☐ white
- ☐ yellow
- ☐ orange
- ☐ gray
- ☐ green
- ☐ brown
- ☐ other

WHAT DID I LEARN ABOUT MYSELF FROM THIS DREAM?

RATING MY STRESS THIS WEEK:

low 1 2 3 4 5 6 7 8 9 10 high

RECORD

DATE ___/___/___ SLEPT FROM ___:___-___:___

LAST NIGHT I DREAMT . . .

REFLECT

THINK THIS DREAM MEANS . . .

3 MAJOR THEMES IN MY DREAM:

MY NIGHTTIME ROUTINE INCLUDED:

- ☐ meditation
- ☐ self-care
- ☐ exercise
- ☐ social media
- ☐ friends/family
- ☐ alcohol
- ☐ reading
- ☐ work
- ☐ other

DID THIS DREAM REMIND ME OF ANYTHING IN MY PAST?

RATING MY MOOD WAKING UP:

poor 1 2 3 4 5 6 7 8 9 10 excellent

RECORD

DATE ___/___/___ SLEPT FROM ___:___-___:___

LAST NIGHT I DREAMT . . .

REFLECT

THINK THIS DREAM MEANS . . .

SETTINGS IN MY DREAM:

NIGHTS I'VE HAD DREAMS THIS WEEK:

- ☐ Monday
- ☐ Tuesday
- ☐ Wednesday
- ☐ Thursday
- ☐ Friday
- ☐ Saturday
- ☐ Sunday

WHAT STOOD OUT MOST IN MY DREAM?

RATING MY ENJOYMENT OF MY DREAM:

poor 1 2 3 4 5 6 7 8 9 10 excellent

RECORD

DATE ___/___/___ SLEPT FROM ___:___-___:___

LAST NIGHT I DREAMT . . .

REFLECT

I THINK THIS DREAM MEANS . . .

3 QUOTES FROM MY DREAM:

THIS DREAM REMINDED ME OF:

- ☐ childhood
- ☐ work
- ☐ friends
- ☐ relationships
- ☐ family
- ☐ other

HOW HAVE I BEEN FEELING OVER THE PAST FEW DAYS?

RATING HOW REALISTIC OR SURREAL MY DREAM FELT:

very realistic 1 2 3 4 5 6 7 8 9 10 very surreal

RECORD

DATE ___/___/___ SLEPT FROM ___:___-___:___

LAST NIGHT I DREAMT . . .

REFLECT

I THINK THIS DREAM MEANS . . .

3 SYMBOLS IN MY DREAM:

THIS DREAM TOOK PLACE:

- ☐ at home
- ☐ at work/school
- ☐ in nature
- ☐ in the city
- ☐ in an abstract place
- ☐ unknown
- ☐ other

WHAT WAS THE MOST UNUSUAL OR SURREAL PART OF MY DREAM?

RATING THE INTENSITY OF EMOTIONS (GOOD OR BAD) IN MY DREAM:

minimal 1 2 3 4 5 6 7 8 9 10 overwhelming

RECORD

DATE ___/___/___ SLEPT FROM ___:___-___:___

LAST NIGHT I DREAMT . . .

REFLECT

I THINK THIS DREAM MEANS . . .

THE DAY BEFORE MY DREAM CONSISTED OF:

- ☐ time outdoors
- ☐ work/school
- ☐ self-care
- ☐ time with friends/family
- ☐ chores
- ☐ downtime
- ☐ other

3 SIGNIFICANT COLORS IN MY DREAM:

WHAT KINDS OF DREAMS DO I WISH I HAD MORE OFTEN?

RATING THE CLARITY OF MY DREAM:

vague 1 2 3 4 5 6 7 8 9 10 extremely vivid

RECORD

DATE ___/___/___ SLEPT FROM ___:___-___:___

LAST NIGHT I DREAMT . . .

REFLECT

I THINK THIS DREAM MEANS . . .

3 SIGNIFICANT OBJECTS IN MY DREAM:

THIS DREAM INCLUDED:

- ☐ people
- ☐ animals
- ☐ dialogue
- ☐ nature
- ☐ strong emotions
- ☐ fantasy elements
- ☐ other

WHAT WAS THE MAIN EMOTION I FELT IN THIS DREAM?

RATING MY MOOD BEFORE BEDTIME:

poor 1 2 3 4 5 6 7 8 9 10 excellent

RECORD

DATE ___/___/___ SLEPT FROM ___:___-___:___

LAST NIGHT I DREAMT . . .

REFLECT

I THINK THIS DREAM MEANS . . .

3 POSSIBLE LESSONS FROM MY DREAM:

THIS DREAM INSPIRES ME TO:

- ☐ evaluate relationships
- ☐ take better care of myself
- ☐ advance my career
- ☐ improve sleep
- ☐ reduce stress
- ☐ other

WHAT PHYSICAL SENSATIONS DID I EXPERIENCE IN MY DREAM?

RATING MY WORK-LIFE BALANCE LATELY:

poor 1 2 3 4 5 6 7 8 9 10 excellent

RECORD

DATE ___/___/___ SLEPT FROM ___:___ - ___:___

LAST NIGHT I DREAMT . . .

REFLECT

I THINK THIS DREAM MEANS . . .

3 ACTIONS I TOOK IN MY DREAM:

THIS DREAM WAS:

- ☐ recurring
- ☐ surreal
- ☐ realistic
- ☐ enjoyable
- ☐ unpleasant
- ☐ long
- ☐ short
- ☐ other

DID MY DREAM HAVE A RESOLUTION OR DID IT FEEL UNFINISHED?

RATING THE SUPPORT SYSTEM CURRENTLY AROUND ME:

poor 1 2 3 4 5 6 7 8 9 10 excellent

RECORD

DATE ___/___/___ SLEPT FROM ___:___-___:___

LAST NIGHT I DREAMT . . .

REFLECT

I THINK THIS DREAM MEANS . . .

3 PEOPLE WHO WERE IN MY DREAM:

THIS DREAM MADE ME FEEL:

- ☐ happy
- ☐ angry
- ☐ sad
- ☐ confused
- ☐ scared
- ☐ other

HOW DOES THIS DREAM RELATE TO MY LIFE?

RATING MY QUALITY OF SLEEP:

poor 1 2 3 4 5 6 7 8 9 10 excellent

RECORD

DATE ____/____/____ SLEPT FROM ____:____-____:____

LAST NIGHT I DREAMT . . .

REFLECT

I THINK THIS DREAM MEANS . . .

3 WORDS TO DESCRIBE MY DREAM:

COLORS IN MY DREAM:

- ☐ red
- ☐ pink
- ☐ black
- ☐ blue
- ☐ purple
- ☐ white
- ☐ yellow
- ☐ orange
- ☐ gray
- ☐ green
- ☐ brown
- ☐ other

WHAT DID I LEARN ABOUT MYSELF FROM THIS DREAM?

RATING MY STRESS THIS WEEK:

low 1 2 3 4 5 6 7 8 9 10 high

RECORD

DATE ___/___/___ SLEPT FROM ___:___ - ___:___

LAST NIGHT I DREAMT . . .

REFLECT

THINK THIS DREAM MEANS . . .

MAJOR THEMES IN MY DREAM:

MY NIGHTTIME ROUTINE INCLUDED:

- ☐ meditation
- ☐ self-care
- ☐ exercise
- ☐ social media
- ☐ friends/family
- ☐ alcohol
- ☐ reading
- ☐ work
- ☐ other

ID THIS DREAM REMIND ME OF ANYTHING IN MY PAST?

RATING MY MOOD WAKING UP:

poor 1 2 3 4 5 6 7 8 9 10 excellent

An Imprint of MandalaEarth
PO Box 3088
San Rafael, CA 94912
www.MandalaEarth.com

Publisher Raoul Goff
Associate Publisher Roger Shaw
Senior Editor Peter Behravesh
Assistant Editor Amanda Nelson
Creative Director Ashley Quackenbush
Senior Designer Stephanie Odeh
VP Manufacturing Alix Nicholaeff
Print Production Manager Tiffani Patterson
Strategic Production Planner Lina s Palma-Temena

ISBN: 979-8-8876-2160-9

Manufactured in China by Insight Editions

10 9 8 7 6 5 4 3 2 1

Insight Editions, in association with Roots of Peace, will plant two trees for each tree used in the manufacturing of this book. Roots of Peace is an internationally renowned humanitarian organization dedicated to eradicating land mines world-wide and converting war-torn lands into productive farms and wildlife habitats. Roots of Peace will plant two million fruit and nut trees in Afghanistan and provide farmers there with the skills and support necessary for sustainable land use.